YOU CAN BEGIN AGAIN

Rebuilding When Life Has Torn You Down

Christopher C. Moore

WESTBOW
PRESS®
A DIVISION OF THOMAS NELSON
& ZONDERVAN

WestBow Press books may be ordered through booksellers or by contacting:

WestBow Press
A Division of Thomas Nelson & Zondervan
1663 Liberty Drive
Bloomington, IN 47403
www.westbowpress.com
1 (866) 928-1240

ISBN: 978-1-9736-2431-8 (sc)
ISBN: 978-1-9736-2430-1 (e)

Library of Congress Control Number: 2018903983

Print information available on the last page.

WestBow Press rev. date: 04/03/2018

Praise of Christopher Moore

We can't avoid tragedy on our life's journey, but we can make the most from them. Tragedy is universal. All of us face tragedy and disappointments in life for it is common to mankind. "Wherever you are and whoever you are your tragedy is not your undoing," says Christopher Moore in his book *You Can Begin Again*. The author, who is a trusted friend of mine, offers solid hope and comfort to those who are facing some of life's greatest challenges.

It seems to me that most of the news I read, watch, and hear is terribly discouraging because it reports one tragedy after another. We are living in tough times, and everybody you meet is facing something and searching for answers. These messages from Rev. Christopher Moore's book will bring you encouragement as he explores some of the great components of Nehemiah's God-centered leadership that fueled him to complete the rebuilding project of the walls in Jerusalem.

With wisdom straight from God's Word, these messages will hopefully guide you through your difficult times and encourage *you to begin again.* Just as God empowered Nehemiah, He can do the same for you.

The Israelites said, "There is so much rubble that we cannot rebuild the wall." That's frustration. They were disheartened and frustrated over what seemed to be an impossible situation. They lost sight of their goal because there was so much junk in their lives that they didn't know how to get to the real business of living. *You Can Begin Again* is a must-read for this day and times.

Rev. Christopher Moore helps you to rediscover (or perhaps discover for the first time) an optimistic outlook on life that can help you face each challenge that confront you. He helps you to trust in God's Word again. Take control of your journey again with the insights and encouragement from his book.

—Dr. Samuel Jackson Gilbert, Sr.
Pastor Emeritus, Mt. Sinai Baptist Church, Houston, Texas

Pastor Christopher Moore opens our hearts and minds to Nehemiah's God-centered leadership, which started with a prayer of repentance after he heard about the condition of the city and the wall of Jerusalem being broken down, gates burned, and the city laid in ruin. Nehemiah started with fasting and prayer before the God of heaven. In his prayer there is praise, for he beseeched God as the God of heaven, the great and terrible God that keeps covenant and mercy for them who loved Him. Nehemiah petitioned God to hear his prayer with an attentive ear and with eyes open. He prayed night and day for the children of Israel. While praying, confession was made for the children of Israel's sins and his own.

Pastor Moore wants us to know that our beginning again must start with God. God empowered Nehemiah, and He will empower us. Also, this book teaches us that God-centered leadership starts with God and continues with Him, trusting and depending on Him to help us rise from the dust of tragedy or the ruins of the storms of life. With our trust in God we can begin again.

Thanks to Pastor Moore for his insight on how Nehemiah trusted God while fighting against obstacles and barriers, continuing to work, and ultimately being successful because he never stopped trusting in God. This book reveals, through Pastor Moore, how a continual trust in God can keep us going after we begin again. I highly recommend that everyone read this book because we never know when we may need to start over.

—Pastor George Cartwright
Pastor, Mt. Horeb Baptist Church, San Augustine, Texas

If you want to deepen your walk and sharpen your leadership skills, then immerse yourself in the principles of this book. It is not just biblical but also practical situations that will allow you to have a fresh start regardless of what stage of life you are in. With simple yet profound insights, this book instructs followers of Christ to trust God when life consumes you. Pastor Moore in this book gives us a greater insight that can help us to start over and start afresh with biblical concepts. The biblical principles that Pastor Moore expounds upon in this book will empower believers and help us to become better leaders for the kingdom. We thank God for the man of God who takes the time to give some insight and instructions on how we can start again.

—Pastor Charles W. Gaines, Sr.
Pastor, New Spirit of Life Baptist Church, Houston, Texas

Contents

Foreword

The image of a wall is an archetype understood in every culture and for millennia past.

The poet laureate Robert Frost wrote the poem "Mending Wall" as a tribute to President John Fitzgerald for his inauguration. The last line of Frost's poem reads, "Good fences make for good neighbors."

The Blues singer Little Milton wrote a song titled "If Walls Could Talk," and he told how they would tell you a lot of things that you wouldn't want them to say. Around the world, walls have their own story to tell.

- The Great Wall of China can be seen from space as can the remains of Hadrian's Roman Wall in England. It tells the story of separation.
- The Berlin Wall marks our time as the greatest gash in Berlin. People died when they were caught in the barbed wire of no man's land as they were trying to get over the wall. That wall tells the story of division.
- The Wailing Wall is where millions of Christians take their annual pilgrimage to pray at the wall of devotion.
- The Vietnam Memorial Wall is a sad wall. Its stones carry the names of the dead. It is the wall of commemoration.

The walls of a city bore witness to the god of the city. Look back to the walls of Babylon. The great city of the ancient world was known for its walls. They were wide enough for two chariots to ride side by side on the top. But today they are gone. The walls of the Roman Empire are cracked and broken. They too are gone. Babylon, Rome, and Athens were surrounded by the protection of their massive walls. But today all those walls lay in ruin. When the walls are down, the witness is down.

Yet in 445 BC, a Jewish layman and contemporary of Aristotle and Plato did what no one thought possible of doing. He returned to his home country and galvanized a group of dispirited Israelites. They showed up like a lightning bolt and did what they didn't think they could do. In the spirit of Nehemiah, we, too, can join hands and hearts to build to the glory of God a wall of witness.

We can build the wall of witness when the leadership feels the need.

Nehemiah lived in Susa, the capital city of the Media-Persian Empire, the Washington, DC, of the day. More importantly, the Jews recognized Susa as the capital of the known world at the time. It was a hub of activity, the place of ultimate decision-making. Often breaking news of the empire came to King Artaxerxes's attention through the lips of his cupbearer. Nehemiah was the king's right-hand man.

During the winter month of December 445–444 BC, Nehemiah was visited by his brother, Hananai, and some men from Judah. And Nehemiah asked them two questions—(1) concerning the Jews who had escaped and had survived the captivity and (2) concerning Jerusalem.

It has been said that a true Jew never completely forgets Jerusalem. This was certainly true of Nehemiah. He wanted to know about the people; he wanted to know the conditions of the beloved city. Those returning from Judah told him, "The people there in the province who survived the captivity are in great distress and reproach."

The people who were in that city were in a vulnerable position. In fact, the men there were under reproach. The Hebrew word means "sharp cutting, penetrating, or piercing." The idea is one bearing the brunt of cutting words. The Jews were being criticized and slandered by people who were enemies of the faith.

Nehemiah was brokenhearted. I'm deeply impressed that though Nehemiah was a high-ranking position in the world, he had a heart that was very tender toward God. It's a tough combination to find a person who holds a high position in the eyes of the world and yet remains tender before God.

When Nehemiah heard the report, he felt the need. What is the level of your concern for the church today? Does it matter to you that we are faced with the most critical decision that we will face for our future? Where is your heart today?

When Nehemiah heard the news of the wall of Jerusalem being torn down, he wept. He wept when he remembered Zion. He wept when he remembered the worship of God. He wept when he reflected on the words of the Torah. He wept as he recalled the stories of his faith. The tears fell from the eyes of Nehemiah all because the wall of protection that stood as a witness to God was gone. In the midst of tears, he fasted and prayed before the God of heaven.

Sjogren's syndrome is an autoimmune deficiency that is characterized by the lack of saliva and an inadequate supply of water to the eyes. It is often characterized by one's inability to shed tears. We don't want to shed artificial tears. We want to weep because we feel a burden for this community. Here is a man who worked his way up from the refugee camps to the king's palace and became an upper-middle-class employee in Susa. His position alone could have kept his from feeling the needs of his people back home. Still, he kept the love of his country dear to his heart and wept when he heard that the wall of his home city was torn down.

There are some today who will say, "We have members. Let them weep. I have my own problems. I'm up to my neck in debt. I can't pay attention to another need." But we can build a wall of witness for this community. The real question before us today is as follows: Does it matter to you? Fathers, does it matter to you? Mothers, does it matter to you? Married couples, does it matter to you? Singles, does it matter to you? Children, does it matter to you? Young adults, does it matter to you? It's a question that only you can answer. If you can ask God today to help you feel the need, you will be the catalyst to starting over. In the movie *The Field of Dreams*, one character says as the hook to the movie, "If you build it, they will come." That's not what our purpose is. Our purpose is thus: If we feel it, we will build it.

We build the *walls of witness* because we desire to begin again!

—Rev. Dr. Ralph Douglas West, Sr.
Pastor, The Church without Walls, Houston, Texas

Acknowledgments

To God be the glory for allowing me this long-desired opportunity to present my thoughts in the form of a published work. Even as I write this portion of the book at this very moment, I can't help but to think about how proud my late parents would be about this achievement. Robert and Dorothy Moore, thank you for the great sacrifices that you made to ensure that I was raised in the fear and admonition of our Lord and that I could attend great institutions of learning to foster my creative development. You always taught me to give everything my very best shot. That along with my Christian upbringing, which still holds me this very moment, fuels me daily.

To my family, thank you for your support and encouragement along the way. I can't imagine my life without any of you. Your support isn't a new thing. You've supported me my entire life. I have been blessed to be surrounded by the most outstanding siblings in the entire world—Doranesia, Chemetri, Sharon, and Erick—and wonderful aunts, uncles, a nephew, nieces, and cousins. You're the best.

I've met some very special friends along life's journey, and they have literally saved my life. I can't thank you enough for holding me accountable, imparting strength when I was weak, and pushing me when I didn't think I had anything left. My life is the richer because you've been there for me every step of the way.

Thanks so much to my pastors—Pastor Cartwright, Dr. Nash, and Pastor Gaines—for the pastoral wisdom that you've poured into me throughout the years. Not only did you teach me what it means to be an effective preacher/pastor, but you've given me lessons that are so instrumental in my development as a man. I have no idea where I would be if it were not for your guidance.

To each pastor and congregation that has allowed me to practice my craft throughout the years, I thank you for being concerned enough about me to invest in me as a student, preacher, pastor, and person. You have encouraged me, and you have supported me. I will be forever grateful for your investments.

Lastly, thank you, New Mount Calvary Baptist Church, for your prayers and support during this entire process. I am grateful to God to pastor such a wonderful congregation that fully supports efforts such as this. We've grown together in grace in these short years that we've shared, and I trust God that our partnership will only flourish in the days ahead.

My prayer is that God continues to richly bless each of you. Grace and peace be unto you.

Introduction

Before the video gaming industry's technology advanced to the heights of this current day, others of my generation and I were subjected to block-like characters and choppy game play. Of course, that wasn't the perception of the gaming consoles at the time. The Super Nintendo console was the best thing since sliced bread.

I spent countless hours attempting to conquer the highest level or capture the league championship. I unashamedly spent a lot of time of playing because I enjoyed it so much, but despite my seeming infatuation with the console, the most frustrating thing about my sixteen-bit Super Nintendo system was that seemingly when I was close to mastering the game, it would suddenly freeze up without any possibility of saving my progress. The only alternative was to hit the dreaded reset button and start all over again.

What a frustrating result! I had spent so much time, and I had nothing to show for it. As a matter of fact, it was so frustrating that it seemed easier to quit the game altogether without even the thought of starting over again because there was always the chance that the same unfortunate circumstance would happen again.

Unfortunately for all of us, life will become choppy and freeze up like a sixteen-bit video game. The truth of the matter is that at some time or another, life will happen on such an overwhelming front that it will seem easier for you to just quit as opposed to pushing the reset button on your life and attempting to regroup and begin again. Spouses will cheat. Relationships will dissolve. Employers will terminate. Finances will plummet. Loved ones will die. Racists will oppress. Dreams will be denied. Businesses will crumble. Automobiles will be repossessed. Health will deteriorate. Moral failure will occur.

Often, in reference to the unfavorable circumstances of life, we hear that there is no reset button, and although it is true that we cannot jump into the proverbial time machine to go back and redo life's darkest moments, with the help of God, we can rebound and rebuild in the face of life's tragedies.

When I endeavored to write on the subject matter of rebuilding after life has torn you down, I admittedly had very little life experience pertaining to the subject matter. I only had a model of encouragement from the leadership principles of Nehemiah in how he not only rebuilt the walls but also rebuilt the people. It was encouraging to read through his personal memoirs of how he continually led the people with strategic excellence and an unwavering trust in God, but little did I know that I would have to simultaneously live through a personal tragedy and help a congregation respond to tragedy on a corporate level just as Nehemiah did.

What does a believer do in a situation such as this? Better yet, what does a young, inexperienced, first-time pastor do in the face of the sudden loss of his mother to cancer and the task of moving a fractured congregation past a painful church split? Well, in an attempt not to be too shallow in my answer, I'll tell you what I did. I simply trusted God to do for me what I was unable to do in my own strength. That was the lesson that I learned from this mighty leader in the Old Testament.

Just as Nehemiah encouraged himself and the people that they could begin again, I did the same for me and the congregation that I'm afforded the opportunity to pastor. The key was trusting God to remove the fear of potentially being disappointed by the same hurts again. That's still the key even today.

That truth is not limited to me only. *You* can trust God to help you move forward from the tragedies of life that have left you reeling. Your confidence should lie in the fact that the same God that has kept you in past experiences will be there to carry you even as you move forward.

But I want to preface that rebuilding when life has torn you down will not be without its share of obstacles and opposition along the way, but your faith in God will propel you above the place where fear once hindered you. So I say to you, the pastor, ministry leader, layperson, spouse, child, friend, employee, or business owner, "No matter what, you can begin again."

Maybe you've lost a loved one, but you can begin again. Maybe you've been terminated from a longtime employer, but you can begin again. Maybe you've been devastated by a horrendous natural disaster, but you can begin again. Maybe you've suffered through an ugly divorce, but you can begin again. Maybe you're a leader standing before a fractured congregation, but you can still begin again.

Whatever scope of life you're in, you can trust God to empower you to restart and rebuild your life when circumstances have torn you down. Yes, you can begin again.

CHAPTER
1

When It All Falls Down

The words of Nehemiah the son of Hachaliah. It came to pass in the month of Chislev, in the twentieth year, as I was in Shushan the citadel,

that Hanani one of my brethren came with men from Judah; and I asked them concerning the Jews who had escaped, who had survived the captivity, and concerning Jerusalem.

And they said to me, "The survivors who are left from the captivity in the province are there in great distress and reproach. The wall of Jerusalem is also broken down, and its gates are burned with fire."

So it was, when I heard these words, that I sat down and wept, and mourned for many days; I was fasting and praying before the God of heaven.

And I said: "I pray, Lord God of heaven, O great and awesome God, You who keep Your covenant and mercy with those who love You and observe Your commandments,

please let Your ear be attentive and Your eyes open, that You may hear the prayer of Your servant which I pray before You now, day and night, for the children of Israel Your servants, and confess the sins of the children of Israel which we have sinned against You. Both my father's house and I have sinned.

We have acted very corruptly against You, and have not kept the commandments, the statutes, nor the ordinances which You commanded Your servant Moses.

Remember, I pray, the word that You commanded Your servant Moses, saying, 'If you are unfaithful, I will scatter you among the nations;

but if you return to Me, and keep My commandments and do them, though some of you were cast out to the farthest part of the heavens, yet I will gather them from there, and bring them to the place which I have chosen as a dwelling for My name.'

Now these are Your servants and Your people, whom You have redeemed by Your great power, and by Your strong hand.

O Lord, I pray, please let Your ear be attentive to the prayer of Your servant, and to the prayer of Your servants who desire to fear Your name; and let Your servant prosper this day, I pray, and grant him mercy in the sight of this man." For I was the king's cupbearer.

—Nehemiah 1:1–11 (NKJV)

On the morning of September 11, 2001, nineteen al-Qaeda terrorists hijacked four commercial passenger jet airliners. The hijackers intentionally crashed two of the airliners into the Twin Towers of the World Trade Center in New York City, killing everyone on board and many others working in the building. Both buildings collapsed within two hours, destroying nearby buildings and damaging others. The hijackers crashed a third airliner into the Pentagon in Arlington, Virginia, just outside of Washington, DC, while the fourth plane crashed into a field near Shanksville in rural Pennsylvania.

In total, almost three thousand people died in the attacks, marking one of the most devastating and debilitating incidents in world history. No matter how much time passes, the memories and stinging effects of this event are as fresh as this morning's newspaper. Its effect is doubly damaging because this event hit close to home. It affected some of our fellow countrymen. Someone's mother or father, someone's husband or wife, or someone's son or daughter lost his or her life to a cold and heinous attack. For all involved, everything had fallen down.

We've all experienced these moments, and although our moments may not have been as extreme as 9/11, we've had moments in our lives that have left us with looming questions. How do we get ourselves together after tragedy strikes? But it's not *if* tragedy strikes. It's *when* tragedy strikes. We cannot ignore the inevitability of trials, and this is inclusive of those of the faith.

The epitome of life falling down is a free-falling, a seemingly nonstop set of sudden and severe circumstances.

- It's a second or third bout of cancer.
- It's dealing with the loss of one parent on the heels of losing the other parent just months prior.
- It's having to bury a newborn child after countless complications.
- It's a sudden job termination in the face of a financial crisis.
- It's the dismay of dealing with the loss of a loved one to some heinous crime after numerous reports across the nation of the same type of crime.
- It's the constant, depressing battle of dealing with uncooperative congregants while attempting to do ministry.

This isn't new. It's old news that's as difficult today to accept as it's ever been. Simply put, bad news finds us whether we're looking for it or not, and at the end of the day, we must determine how we will respond when life has torn us down.

Nehemiah, the governor of the province of Judah, shows us this truth in practice through his personal memoirs in thirteen chapters dealing with the restoration of the walls in Jerusalem. They had lain in ruins since 586 BC as a result of Nebuchadnezzar breaching them, taking the Jews into Babylonian captivity, and burning the temple. Consequently, the few Jews who remained could not defend themselves, and the returned exiles attempted to rebuild the walls in or shortly after 458 BC. However, they were unable to do so.

Nehemiah had been serving at the Persian winter palace in Susa, and one day he received a report from several men, including his brother, Hanani. When he received the news about the plight of his people, he was emotionally pained because they were now left without protection.

So Nehemiah then finds himself in the midst of a falling moment, and he must determine how he will handle this crisis. This is the lesson for all of us as well. We must meet great tragedy with a godly response. So the question lies before us. How do we respond when all that is seemingly stable around us crumbles and falls down?

Control Your Emotional State in the Midst of Bad News

A Methodist preacher by the name of Luther Bridges was married and had three sons. Pastor Bridges accepted an invitation to minister at a conference in Kentucky, so he left his family in the care of his father-in-law and made the trip to Kentucky. There, he gave two wonderful weeks of ministry. The last service closed with great joy, and he was excited to be called to the telephone. He couldn't wait to tell his wife about all the blessings.

But to his dismay, it wasn't her voice on that long-distance call. He listened in both shock and silence to the news. A fire had burned down the house of his father-in-law, and his wife and all three of his sons had died in the blaze. This was sudden, but worse still, it was severe. For Bridges, the bottom had fallen out.

When Nehemiah heard the dismal report about the deplorable state of his fellow countrymen, it sent his emotional state into a sudden downward spiral. He sat down, wept, and mourned for many days. This was not just a mere exhibition of emotion. This was an outward and inward pain that penetrated his soul. This was not any old bad news. It was news that hit close to home. He had learned of the Jews' unsuccessful attempts to rebuild Jerusalem's walls, leaving his native people defenseless against hostile neighbors and vulnerable to the enemy.

And what bad news this must've been to Nehemiah. His people were not only disarmed but seemingly left on their own! Even after these Jews had escaped from Babylonian captivity, it still did them no good to return because the place they were returning to was now destroyed. They went from being in bondage in Babylon to now being in worse shape. The city they once knew was gone.

But it was not Nehemiah avoiding mourning and grieving that was so admirable. It was the way in which he handled his emotions after receiving such bad news He did not allow his emotional state to overwhelm him so much that it took his focus off God.

We must also understand this attitude. Weeping did not make Nehemiah less spiritual. Nor did it make him weak. Weeping did not diminish his trust in God. On so many occasions, we are scolded within the Christian community for mourning great losses as if we are superhuman and not supposed to mourn. Crying is frowned upon because it reveals the kinks in our armor; however, our very own Savior wept on the heels of a personal loss in John 11:35, and if He wept, then we are permitted to weep in the face of great trials. But we should not weep as if all is hopeless.

All of us have received earth-shattering news, but how do we handle it? That's the question that stands before each of us in life's tough moments. I've discovered that there are usually two groups of people when it comes to how they handle their emotional states in the midst of bad news. There are those who can't see God because of their problems, and then there are those who can't see their problems because of God. Don't magnify your problems so much that you minimize God's effectiveness to handle your problems. We may be powerless against the nature of the circumstance, but we have the power to control our response to the circumstance. How can that be? Does it come by trusting in things or by trusting in other people? No, it comes by trusting in the fact that we can trust God in the midst of the circumstance. That's where your focus should be in the midst of bad news, and that's where you can find strength.

Converse with the Father through Prayer

Once again, remember that we will all experience what Nehemiah experienced at some point. Life around us will crumble, and it won't be a pleasant feeling; however,, those circumstances shouldn't drive us to a pity party. They should drive us to a prayer meeting. After Nehemiah wept and mourned, he then fasted and prayed.

Nehemiah's fasting and praying was constant. He prayed both day and night. Nehemiah knew that he could only ease his troubled soul and address his problems through a healthy prayer relationship with God. This was the key. His prayer life was not some secondary action that he resorted to when things were not going well, but prayer was a priority in his everyday life.

Prayer was not for his idle amusement. It was not some casual encounter with the Father, but it was an intimate time in which he voiced his reverential adoration for God. It was not merely a survey of requests of what he needed. Prayer was a priority because Nehemiah reveled in the fact that this was a time for him to get closer to the Father. This was not a first-time affair for Nehemiah. This was not just a routine. It was an all-day, everyday occurrence.

Nehemiah did not confine his prayers to circumstance, but instead he expressed his desire to commune and converse with the Father. This was not just Nehemiah talking to God, but it was an opportunity for God to talk to him as well. And the heart of our prayer ought to be a constant desire to commune with God in every situation.

As matter of fact, we ought to tend to every whim and every situation through the act of prayer. Abraham Lincoln once declared, "I've been driven to my knees on so many occasions by the circumstances of life, that I determined that I had nowhere else to go."

Unfortunately, some people don't understand the necessity of prayer, so they don't pray until circumstances *call for them do so.* But our prayer lives should not be confined to an occasional Hail Mary. We must undersand that prayer is the sustaining factor in our lives when times become rough; the potent process that changes people, personalities, and situations; and the way in which we tell our heavenly Father that we worship and need Him.

All circumstances are just more opportunities to pray!

For the sake of emphasis, I've included one of the great prayers recorded in the Bible that we really cannot ignore. This is a clear example of the type of prayer that God answers in the affirmative—if it is in His divine will to do so.

Reverent Prayer

Before Nehemiah asks God for anything, he firstly reveres God for who He is. He publicly acknowledges God as worthy of this type of fervent prayer. From the start, this teaches us that we shouldn't go to God without revering Him for who He is. He is our great and awesome God.

He calls Him "Lord," which points to the Lord's covenant relationship with His people. He is a God that never leaves or forsakes. We are only able to connect to Him because He's obligated Himself to connect to us.

Nehemiah also calls Him "the God of heaven," which points to His sovereignty. The Lord can literally do what He wants to, when He wants to do it, where He wants to do it, and how He wants to do it. He is the God over both heaven and earth.

This man then calls Him a "great and awesome God," which points to the Lord's power and majesty. Nehemiah essentially admits that the Lord is able. That's why *we* depend upon Him. At the end of the day, when we pray, we are showing God that we depend upon Him because we know who He is. We should *always* thank Him for what He's done, but we must never forget who He is. Nehemiah shows us that no prayer should leave out a reverential adoration for God. In other words, no prayer should leave out God.

Prayer isn't predicated upon what's going on around us. Prayer is predicated upon the great God that is above us. Friends, no matter what, don't allow circumstances to distort who He is.

Penitent Prayer

After revering who God is, Nehemiah moves to the heart of the prayer. He confesses day and night his sins and the sins of his fellow people before God. He doesn't attempt to present himself to God as something that he's not. He is sincerely real before God. He included the sins of the people, and therefore, he doesn't leave himself out.

As the prophet Daniel had prayed almost a hundred years before and as Ezra had also prayed, Nehemiah acknowledged that he shared responsibility for Israel's disobedience to God's laws. We ought to be *that* honest with God. After all, we have sinned against Him. Whether or not we confess our sins to anyone, God knows that we've sinned against Him.

We *must* confess our sinfulness to God, not only because it is mandatory but because the Lord forgives us. First John 1:9 declares, "If you confess your sins, He is faithful and just to forgive you and cleanse you from all unrighteousness."

Once, an Italian duke walked aboard a galley ship. As he passed the crew of slaves, he asked several of them what their offenses were. Every one blamed someone else, saying that his brother was to blame or that the judge was bribed. One sturdy young fellow said, "My lord, I am justly in here. I wanted money, and I stole it. No one is to blame but myself." When the duke heard this, he seized the man by the shoulder and said, "You rogue! What are you doing here among so many honest men? Get you out of their company!" In actuality, the young fellow was then set free, while the rest were left to tug at the oars. That's what unconfessed sins do. They literally leave us tugging at the oars while we could be free through confession and repentance.

But because Nehemiah is real before God, he's able to remind God of a promise that He'd previously made. He doesn't remind God of the promise because God has forgotten but because he wants God to act upon his behalf. He reminds God of the promise that He made to Moses. Just as the Lord would disperse them from their homeland if the nation was unfaithful, those who were exiled would be regathered to Jerusalem if they obeyed Him. This was predicated upon their obedience to God. They had finally come to grips that they were wrong and God was right the entire time. If we come clean with God, He will move the obstacles out of the way so that we can remember His promises.

What sins are hindering you from remembering God's promises? Whatever they are, confession and repentance can reestablish you and place you on the right path.

Continue to Hope in the Sovereignty of God

Nehemiah knew that if the walls were to be restored in Jerusalem, it would take much prayer and faith in God. He hoped that beseeching God would not fall upon deaf ears, so he prayed in faith that God would act on behalf of his people and allow him the opportunity rebuild both the walls and the people.

But only King Artazerxes could aid Nehemiah in helping the Jews in Jerusalem. Years earlier the king had issued a decree that ceased the rebuilding efforts in Jerusalem, and he was the only one who could reverse such an order. That's why Nehemiah asked God to grant him favor in the sight of the king.

Four months went by before Nehemiah's opportunity came. He was going about his usual duties as the king's cupbearer when the king noticed that he was pained about something. Nehemiah responded to the king's inquiry by requesting that he return to Jerusalem to tend to his people and rebuild the walls so that they would be safe against enemy attacks. Ironically, the king consented to allow him to rebuild the walls.

This was a sudden turn of events. When man initially said no, God stepped in and said *yes*. God prepared the individual about whom Nehemiah was praying. As God prepared Nehemiah through prayer, He was preparing the king to receive that request. The king became the human instrument for the divine. If you work your prayer life in this manner, it will work for you! More importantly, God will work for you. Nehemiah experienced God's intervention, and you should continue to remember that God's power is always greater than our problems.

I was a student at Dallas Seminary in need of financial assistance for the upcoming semester. Even with a generous gift from an anonymous donor, the remaining balance on my school account exceeded the balance in my bank account. I spoke with the financial aid office, and they notified me that if I didn't pay the remaining balance by the next day, I would be forced to drop all of my classes.

Admittedly, I was fearful and hopeless of a resolution, but I knew that formal seminary training was a part of God's plan for me, so I prayed that God would intervene on my behalf. I went to bed that night, not knowing what tomorrow would hold, but I trusted that God knew what was best. I woke up the next morning and prayed once again that God would intervene on my behalf, and it wasn't very long before I received a call from the financial aid office with news regarding my status. With great joy, I listened to the representative tell me that they would allow me to pay the remaining balance over the course of the semester and that I would be allowed to begin classes as planned. Friends, God is still in the business of saying yes.

CHAPTER
2

It's All in His Hands

And it came to pass in the month of Nisan, in the twentieth year of King Artaxerxes, when wine was before him, that I took the wine and gave it to the king. Now I had never been sad in his presence before.

Therefore the king said to me, "Why is your face sad, since you are not sick? This is nothing but sorrow of heart." So I became dreadfully afraid,

and said to the king, "May the king live forever! Why should my face not be sad, when the city, the place of my fathers' tombs, lies waste, and its gates are burned with fire?"

Then the king said to me, "What do you request?" So I prayed to the God of heaven.

And I said to the king, "If it pleases the king, and if your servant has found favor in your sight, I ask that you send me to Judah, to the city of my fathers' tombs, that I may rebuild it."

Then the king said to me (the queen also sitting beside him), "How long will your journey be? And when will you return?" So it pleased the king to send me; and I set him a time.

Furthermore I said to the king, "If it pleases the king, let letters be given to me for the governors of the region beyond the River, that they must permit me to pass through till I come to Judah,

and a letter to Asaph the keeper of the king's forest, that he must give me timber to make beams for the gates of the citadel which pertains to the temple, for the city wall, and for the house that I will occupy." And the king granted them to me according to the good hand of my God upon me.

Then I went to the governors in the region beyond the River, and gave them the king's letters. Now the king had sent captains of the army and horsemen with me.

When Sanballat the Horonite and Tobiah the Ammonite official heard of it, they were deeply disturbed that a man had come to seek the well-being of the children of Israel.

So I came to Jerusalem and was there three days.

Then I arose in the night, I and a few men with me; I told no one what my God had put in my heart to do at Jerusalem; nor was there any animal with me, except the one on which I rode.

And I went out by night through the Valley Gate to the Serpent Well and the Refuse Gate, and viewed the walls of Jerusalem which were broken down and its gates which were burned with fire.

14Then I went on to the Fountain Gate and to the King's Pool, but there was no room for the animal under me to pass.

So I went up in the night by the valley, and viewed the wall; then I turned back and entered by the Valley Gate, and so returned.

And the officials did not know where I had gone or what I had done; I had not yet told the Jews, the priests, the nobles, the officials, or the others who did the work.

Then I said to them, "You see the distress that we are in, how Jerusalem lies waste, and its gates are burned with fire. Come and let us build the wall of Jerusalem, that we may no longer be a reproach."

And I told them of the hand of my God which had been good upon me, and also of the king's words that he had spoken to me. So they said, "Let us rise

up and build." Then they set their hands to this
good work.

But when Sanballat the Horonite, Tobiah the
Ammonite official, and Geshem the Arab heard
of it, they laughed at us and despised us, and said,
"What is this thing that you are doing? Will you
rebel against the king?"

So I answered them, and said to them, "The God
of heaven Himself will prosper us; therefore we
His servants will arise and build, but you have no
heritage or right or memorial in Jerusalem."

—Nehemiah 2 (NKJV)

There's a story about a boy and his mother shopping in the
neighborhood grocery store. They often shopped at the store,
and they had become quite familiar with the owner. The owner
often noticed how well-behaved and respectful the young man was
toward his mother, and he decided that he wanted to reward the
young man with something special when they were ready to pay
for their items.

Behind the counter, he kept a large bowl of candy, and he would
often give some to the children who were on their best behavior in
the store. This was an opportunity for them to grab as much candy
as they could possibly hold in their hands.

This young man was no exception, and he wanted to extend to
him the same opportunity. And sure enough, once the mother had

paid for her items, the store owner brought the large bowl of candy around to the boy, but he refused to reach into the bowl.

His mother let him know that it was okay for him to get the candy, but he still refused to reach into the bowl. He politely asked the owner if he would grab the candy for him, and the man did just that. To the boy's delight, the man had gathered so much candy that he had to place it in a plastic bag.

Upon walking out of the store, the mother asked her son why he never got the candy out of the jar himself, and he kindly responded, "Mother, I allowed the store owner to grab the candy because his hands are much bigger than mine."

What a lesson in childlike dependance! Instead of trusting in our own capabilities and efforts, we should trust God wholeheartedly. There's absolutely nothing that we can do apart from the power of God, and that includes dealing with the harsh instances of life. The good news is that while things for are too hard for us to handle, there's nothing too hard for Him.

He can handle a wayward child gone wild. He can handle an addiction that you can't seem to shake.He can handle a financial issue that you can't seem to resolve. He can handle an emotional roller coaster that you can't control.He can handle a tumultuous storm that you can't calm. Simply put, when you can't, He can.

That's the tenor of Nehemiah's sentiment at this stage of his personal journey of rebuilding the walls in Jerusalem. He had dealt with the emotional turmoil of the destruction of the walls in Jerusalem. He had prayed unto God for strength, direction, and favor. He had taken his concern before the king in regards to the protection of his fellow countrymen, and he was actually given the permission and the means to go forward with the work; however, now the task ahead of him was to actually match his human effort with divine enablement. After the emotional shaking and quaking was over, he had to do something about what he had prayed unto God. The king *and* God had given him permission to go forward with the work, but he had to trust God while moving forward.

Essentially, a God-directed mandate requires faith, but it also requires action. Trusting God wholeheartedly to help us with a task does not mean that we sit idly by. We must allow God to be God, but we must contribute manpower to the miracle. Putting the task in His hands does not mean that we do nothing, but it does mean that we trust Him enough to give Him the control to lead and assist us with the task.

Prepare for the Path to Recovery

Nehemiah had overcome the emotional aspects of the destruction of the walls, but now what? In order to fully recover emotionally from the distress and finally begin the rebuilding effort, there had to be a means of preparation for the path to ultimate recovery. This would be no small undertaking, and Nehemiah had to adequately prepare for the task at hand. How did he do that?

Regroup for the Journey Ahead

This is the first step, but it is perhaps the most diffcult step of moving forward on the path to recovery. It takes discipline and determination to begin a new path on the heels of tragedy, but even though the sting of the tragedy is still there, you have to prayerfully make plans that will put you in the best position to move forward. Before you set the plans though, you must prepare with prayer. This isn't an overnight process that comes to you suddenly. It's not a process that is devoid of any past hurts or relapses, and it doesn't happen without a struggle. But it's necessary. I cannot stress enough the importance of equipping yourself and those around you with prayer for the unseen road ahead. Observe how Nehemiah handled the unforseen road ahead.

Before Nehemiah did anything concerning the rebuilding project, he recouped from the journey behind him and regrouped for the journey ahead by resting, praying, and planning. He had to carry the weight of the painful news that he'd received, all the while preparing for the impending work, but he could not do so without taking the time to mentally regroup.

It was three whole days before Nehemiah even made an attempt to begin the process. He wouldn't take any action without taking the time to properly plan. He wouldn't make any haphazard decisions because he didn't want them to endanger this once-in-a-lifetime opportunity. One wrong move, and it could've hindered their progress, but that was not the case with Nehemiah. He exhibited a valuable principle. He was beginning on the path to recovery, but he knew how he was going to get there. That was only the result of proper planning coupled with prayer. The old adage is true. If you fail to plan, then you're planning to fail. In a lot of cases, we know where we're attempting to go, but we don't know how exactly how we're going to get there. I offer three key components to an effective path to recovery—prayer, planning, and patience.

I am living by these principles at my current pastorate, which also happens to be my first and only pastorate. In the series of interviews that were conducted prior to my calling, I was asked what my vision for the church would be. I made my very best attempt not to sound silly or uneducated, but out came the best answer that I could muster, "I really don't have one." The pastoral search committee looked puzzled from their faces, but I explained to them two things. First, my vision would only be the vision that God gave me, and second, I would need to be called to the church and have adequate time to best familiarize myself with the intricacies of the culture of the church. I would have to be prayerful during this time, and I would also have to be patient. Ambition and aspirations couldn't supecede the process of preparation if we were to be effective. Don't get me wrong. This was not easy to do, but it was best.

Obviously, I came into this pastorate with the burden of huge expectations. I was the youngster that had come by way of Dallas. I had a top-notch seminary education and a great deal of vitality. I was following a very successful predecessor. I was also young enough to dedicate the prime of my adult life to this one congregation, but most importantly, I was the one who was supposed to move this historic congregation forward on the heels of a very painful church split. Talk about pressure! How could I be patient with these expectations, most of them self-inflicted? I had to hit a home run each Sunday and Wednesday. Members had to join at a rapid pace each week. Finances had to increase, and I had to implement new programs. By the grace of God, most of these things happened, but this short honeymoon period was only the tip of the iceberg. Where were we really headed? I still had no idea.

About halfway into the first year of my pastorate at New Mount Calvary (a little more two years have passed since then), the Lord revealed to me the basis of the vision that He would entrust to me to carry the congregation forward. Although the product was clear, the process was cloudy, which definitely tested my patience! I was ready to take on the world, but still had no clear idea how to get there. Mist was distorting my view, so I knew fog was distorting the view of the congregation as well. But I had to remain prayerful and patient. Thankfully, day by day and week by week, the Lord continues to show me how the vision shall unfold. I look back on the earlier days of my pastorate and realize that I didn't see half the things then that I see now, especially in relation to building relationships, but with prayer, preparation, and patience, the Lord continues to give me a window into His plan.

So wherever you are on the path to recovery, please remain prayerful and patient. Make no mistake about it. God's will is perfect and complete, and His plans have no flaws; however, we must also properly prepare to do His will. We should take no step taken without the consent and endorsement of the almighty God, and that permission comes through the act of prayer. It's hard to understand the will of God if you have not sought Him first, and if you're truly going to move foward on the path to recovery, you must prayerfully seek God and learn how you will do it.

Rid Yourself of Excess Baggage

Nehemiah was strategic in how he planned for the rebuilding effort and how he carefully chose the route that would be most beneficial and most secure. He also had to consider two other major issues that would be instrumental in his plan. He had to fully understand that this was not a solo effort, and he had to be able to identify who he could and could not trust.

First of all, Nehemiah had to be discreet in navigating at night so that the enemy was unaware of his whereabouts, and he could not reveal God's plan to just anyone because they may not have fully understood his purpose. He needed assistance in surveying the damage to the walls; however, he could only take a few men with him, and they had to be men that he could trust. His crowd was limited. He didn't even bring excess animals with him, except for the animal that he rode (and he didn't even need that anymore because there wasn't enough room for he and the animal to pass through the Fountain Gate).

The text is clear, and it speaks to us as well. There are some people in our lives who cannot travel along with us on the path to our destiny. Just as Nehemiah realized, we must realize that we need someone in our corner that we can trust, but we must also be careful of the the team members that accompany us on the path to recovery because it's hard to move forward when you're weighed down by hindrances. Is there anyone or anything in your life that you feel contributes to your excess baggage? Do these people hold you back from going where God is trying to take you? If you want to move forward with that which God has predestined for you, you must rid yourself of excess baggage.

Review the Scene so that You Can Move Forward

Nehemiah had to survey the wreckage of the walls undeterred so that he would be able to fairly assess the damage. Then he would learn exactly what they needed for the rebuilding effort. He had to see it for himself in order to know what the next steps would be. If he had only based his report on hearsay, he would have never been able to move forward with the rebuilding plan, but since he saw it for himself, he could fairly assess the damage. He also learned for certain that it was going to take the power of God to make it possible.

In life, we are constantly bombarded with circumstances that leave emotional scars—bad relationships, finacial losses, job terminations, family feuds, or maybe even church hurts—and we attempt to move post past them by simply discarding them from our memory without properly dealing with them. As difficult as it may seem, you have to face the damage in order to move past it. You can't always do this alone though. Perhaps you need others to help you, but certainly, you need God to help you. This is especially important for pastors and servant leaders to remember as they deal with the pains that sometimes come with ministry.

Leading God's people is no small undertaking. It's a blessing, but it also brings it's share of burdens.

The servant leader prays for others. The servant leader arrives at the office, sometimes with a heavy heart. The servant leader balances the ministry of the church and the ministry of the home, and as much as they would like, they can never be everywhere at the same time.

As superhuman as servant leaders look during the worst of times, and as easy and effortless as they make ministry seem, it's not that simple. They need prayer just as much if not more than the laity. They need encouragement. They need support. They need cooperation. They need faithfulness and commitment from those who would follow them as they follow God. They need a listening ear. Without a doubt, God is with those who serve Him, but they need the help of the people as well. Once again, ministry is no small undertaking.

Duke University's Clergy Health Initiative conducted research about these topics and released these findings. "Anxiety and stress levels among clergy are twice the national average ... A number of factors were found to be powerful predictors of depression and anxiety, most notably job stress."

Depression and suicide rates are at an all-time high amongst pastors, and most of these instances stem from unresolved or ignored emotional issues. Those issues cannot be ignored. You must face those issues in order to move past them. Seek the necessary help, whether it be professional help or an accountability partner or group within the body of Christ. Do what is necessary to foster your healing. Once you get past the hurt, you can then focus on moving forward, but more than that, you can trust God to help you. If you'll trust Him, He'll help you.

Place Your Confidence in God

Nehemiah understood that this task was no small undertaking; he not only had to complete the work, but he also had to convince the inhabitants to assist him. They had to be assured that not only were they in good hands, but that the work was in good hands. They had no worries about the work because Nehemiah had shown them that his confidence was in the Almighty God. He proved this to them in the text.

He Can Handle the Obstacle

Nehemiah mentions the reality of the obstacle as he recounts to the people the condition of Jerusalem. It was in shambles, literally destroyed, but he said to them that they should rebuild the walls so that they would no longer be a dissapointment.

Any good leader is honest with his or her followers about the reality of the obstacles in front of them. This is so essential because if there's no recognition of a problem, there is no foundation for a solution.

But Nehemiah did something here that every spiritual leader must do in the face of difficult times. He stood before them in the midst of a trial and displayed his confidence in God by telling them about the great response to the obstacle that they faced. He said that the good hand of God would enable their hands to do the work. They reasoned that since God's hands were enabling them, then they could overcome the obstacles. Isn't it amazing how the confidence of a leader is transferred to his or her followers?

He Can Handle the Opposition

Finally, the secret was out about Nehemiah's plan, and it did not make everyone happy. Sanballat, Tobiah, and Geshem literally mocked the declaration of the people and the efforts of Nehemiah, but he responded by saying that God would prosper them. Opposition comes frequently against the work and the workers of the kingdom, but it's God that strengthens us when the opposition desires to weaken us. Lady Culross declared, "Since God has put His work into your weak hands, look not for long ease here: You must feel the full weight of your calling: a weak man with a strong God."

Ultimately, when the obstacles and the opposition seem too great for us to handle, we must simply concede control to the one that is able work out life's situations better than we can.

This truth became crystal clear to me one night while I was attempting to connect my new laptop to the internet. I would probably label myself as tech savvy, but on this particular night, my capabalities were no match for this task.

After searching through the manual and performing my own tests, I was left with no other solution but to call the customer support line. I remember so vividly talking to that young man about different troubleshooting strategies, but nothing worked. He finally said, "Allow me to try one more thing, but in order for me to do it, you must take your hands off the keys." I did as he instructed, but something strange happened. My cursor began to move. Boxes began to minimize and maximize, and the then I connected to the internet, all without my involvement. It was all because I took my hands off the keys and allowed someone more capable than me to handle the situation. Whenever you find yourself in a situation that is tougher than you can handle, take your hands off of it and allow the Lord to do for you what you're unable to do yourself.

CHAPTER
3

How to Defeat Discouragement

But it so happened, when Sanballat heard that we were rebuilding the wall, that he was furious and very indignant, and mocked the Jews. And he spoke before his brethren and the army of Samaria, and said, "What are these feeble Jews doing? Will they fortify themselves? Will they offer sacrifices? Will they complete it in a day? Will they revive the stones from the heaps of rubbish—stones that are burned?"

Now Tobiah the Ammonite was beside him, and he said, "Whatever they build, if even a fox goes up on it, he will break down their stone wall."

Hear, O our God, for we are despised; turn their reproach on their own heads, and give them as plunder to a land of captivity! Do not cover their iniquity, and do not let their sin be blotted out from before You; for they have provoked You to anger before the builders.

So we built the wall, and the entire wall was joined together up to half its height, for the people had a mind to work.

Now it happened, when Sanballat, Tobiah, the Arabs, the Ammonites, and the Ashdodites heard that the walls of Jerusalem were being restored and the gaps were beginning to be closed, that they became very angry,

and all of them conspired together to come and attack Jerusalem and create confusion.

Nevertheless we made our prayer to our God, and because of them we set a watch against them day and night.

Then Judah said, "The strength of the laborers is failing, and there is so much rubbish that we are not able to build the wall."

And our adversaries said, "They will neither know nor see anything, till we come into their midst and kill them and cause the work to cease."

So it was, when the Jews who dwelt near them came, that they told us ten times, "From whatever place you turn, they will be upon us."

Therefore I positioned men behind the lower parts of the wall, at the openings; and I set the people according to their families, with their swords, their spears, and their bows.

And I looked, and arose and said to the nobles, to the leaders, and to the rest of the people, "Do not be afraid of them. Remember the Lord, great and awesome, and fight for your brethren, your sons, your daughters, your wives, and your houses."

And it happened, when our enemies heard that it was known to us, and that God had brought their plot to nothing, that all of us returned to the wall, everyone to his work.

So it was, from that time on, that half of my servants worked at construction, while the other half held the spears, the shields, the bows, and wore armor; and the leaders were behind all the house of Judah.

Those who built on the wall, and those who carried burdens, loaded themselves so that with one hand they worked at construction, and with the other held a weapon.

Every one of the builders had his sword girded at his side as he built. And the one who sounded the trumpet was beside me.

Then I said to the nobles, the rulers, and the rest of the people, "The work is great and extensive, and we are separated far from one another on the wall.

Wherever you hear the sound of the trumpet, rally to us there. Our God will fight for us."

So we labored in the work, and half of the men held the spears from daybreak until the stars appeared.

At the same time I also said to the people, "Let each man and his servant stay at night in Jerusalem, that they may be our guard by night and a working party by day."

So neither I, my brethren, my servants, nor the men of the guard who followed me took off our clothes, except that everyone took them off for washing.

—Nehemiah 4 (NKJV)

There's an old story about the day when the devil decided to have a garage sale. On the day of the sale, he set out all of his tools for public inspection, and each was marked with its sale price. There were a treacherous lot of implements—hatred, envy, jealousy, deceit, lust, lying, pride, and so on. Set apart from the rest, though, was a tool seemingly harmless but quite worn and pricey. "What is the name of this tool?" asked one of the customers, pointing it out.

Satan replied, "That is discouragement."

The customer asked, "Why do you have it priced so high?"

Satan responded, "Because it is more useful to me than others. I can pry open and get inside a man's heart with that, even when I cannot get near him with the other tools. It is badly worn because I use it on almost everyone since so few people know that it belongs to me. As worn as it appears, it's still effective."

That's a fictional story, but it carries a relevant truth about discouragement. Discouragement serves a disheartening purpose when one allows it to get the best of them. It is the polar opposite of courage. While courage strengthens the heart, discouragement weakens it. Courage says that you can do something, while discouragement says that you can't. Courage says that you can make it, while discouragement says that you don't have a chance. Courage screams victory, while discouragement screams defeat. Courage says that everything will work out in spite of the outlook, but discouragement declares that the outlook is too bleak for a favorable outcome.

Discouragement penetrates the heart and soul of man (Christian or non-Christian) with the hopes of leaving no hope at all. Discouragement wants you to believe that the doctor's bad report is final. Discouragement wants you to believe that the denial letter from the university is final. Discouragement wants you to believe that the *no* from the employer is final Discouragement wants you to believe that your difficulties in this Christian walk are final.

Its carrier is none other than Satan himself and those who would fall prey to his negative influence. As much as Satan has a target on the hearts of all men, he has an even larger arrow of discouragement that he's waiting to thrust into the heart of those who believe in God. Make no mistake about it, Satan wants to discourage those who have hearts for God and His agenda.

It was no different for Nehemiah in his efforts to rebuild the walls in Jerusalem. He was confronted by those who desired to discourage him and his workers from progressing with the work any further.

As mentioned, we heard from three outspoken, indignant men by the names of Sanballat, Tobiah, and Geshem. They despised Nehemiah for attempting to do God's work. This instance was no different. As the work progressed, so did the attempts of Nehemiah's opposition to halt the work. The more work that they completed, the angrier these men became.

That's really what evil people do. They get mad when you're attempting to do good, and when they see that they can't deter the work, they then attempt to discourage the worker. We must understand that discouragement from the opposition is a foe that all of us must face, but we do not have to face it alone. God helps us defeat it. This narrative makes it clear to us exactly how we can defeat this thing called discouragement.

Pray about Your Opposition

Once Sanballat *heard* the news that the rebuilding project would continue, he became furious and indignant, and then he began to mock the Jews. Even though he was mocking the Jews, this was no laughing matter. The words *furious* and *indignant* suggest that he was burning with rage.

He continued to mock the workers as he gathered his local army from Samaria and asked a series of sarcastic questions, basically minimizing the Jews and suggesting they were *feeble*. (This word likens them to a woman who is no longer able to bear children.) He said this for two reasons. First, he did not want them to finish the work, and second, he did not think that they could actually complete the work. That's why he referenced the fact that the burned stones couldn't be revived. (Once limestone is exposed to intense heat, it becomes unsuitable for building.) In his eyes, they were done. And to make matters worse, Tobiah declared that the construction materials were so flimsy that even a small creature such as a fox could jump on the wall and collapse it all.

But that's usually how discouraging people operate. They criticize those who *can* do because either they can't do what you do or they're not willing to put forth the effort to do it. Because they have no goals or aspirations, they don't want to have them either. They possess a "crab in a barrel" mentality. They're comfortable in remaining at the bottom. They'd much rather pull you down instead of attempting to pull themselves up.

That was Nehemiah's opposition's problem with him. He was willing to do something that they weren't willing to do. And because of that, whatever he did, it was never good enough in their eyes. No matter how skilled you think you are, never allow someone else to determine your worth. It is God and God alone that has determined your talent, and no matter how much or how little it seems to someone else, it is of great value to Him.

This is really the heart of the matter. Once Sanballat and Tobiah made their sarcastic remarks, Nehemiah *never* addressed what they said. He merely talked to God about them. This prayer comes off as very harsh. It's one of those prayers that essentially says, "Get 'em, Lord." We would normally call this an imprecatory prayer that calls down God's judgment upon the unrighteous on behalf of the righteous. Nehemiah did not take their mockery personal. (He took it seriously, but he did not take it personal.). But he figured that if they were mocking God's work, then they were mocking God as well. That was a dangerous thing. No one mocks God and His business and gets away with it. Nehemiah's story helps us understand that even though you can pray *for* something, you can also pray *about* something.

There are some people in life who are so treacherous that you can only pray about them. They're too tough for you to handle, and you can't control them in your own strength. I guarantee if you'll pray *about* them, God can do something *with* them!

Press on in Spite of Your Opposition

This is not a *deep* portion of the narrative at all. It just takes a bit of observation. While the enemy was talking, Nehemiah and his workers *never* allowed it to affect their productivity. They built the wall up to half its height because they had a mind to work. (That term suggests that their heart was in it too.)

Now imagine what would have happened if they had bought into what the opposition was saying about them. If they would've entertained such gossip, they never would have gotten as far as they did. There's great danger in believing what people say about what you can't do, especially when God has already empowered you for the task at hand. You'll do much less when you feed into negativity more. You have to press on in spite of the opposition, and that only comes by having a mind to work.

The mind is a powerful resource. It's the center of logical reasoning. It processes thoughts and then acts upon them. In other words, whether positive or negative, once a thought is in your mind, the result is present in your actions. Proverbs 23:7 is right on target. "So as he thinks in his heart, so is he."

Having a mind to work is a matter of focus. You can either maximize your problems to the point that you minimize your productivity, or you can minimize the focus on the opposition because you've magnified the focus on the opportunity.

In 1953, a fledgling business called Rocket Chemical Company and its staff of three people set out to create a line of rust-prevention solvents and degreasers for use in the aerospace industry. It literally took them forty attempts to perfect their formula. And we still use (and love) the original formula to this very day, known as WD-40. But perhaps what you don't know what WD-40 stands— "Water Displacement, 40th Attempt." What a story of persistence!

What if that small company in San Diego would've stopped trying after the tenth or the twentieth attempt? What about after the thirty-ninth attempt? If they would've given up sooner, they would have never achieved their mission, and the world would have never been known their incredible invention.

For the believer, the Christian walk and ministry is difficult. As a matter of fact, at times it becomes so difficult that it can make even the strongest and faithful believers want to throw in the proverbial towel. But if we gave up, we'd be quitting on the God-given mandate of making disciples, and furthermore, we would deprive a dark world of the light of the Lord. The world is wicked, but we can't quit trying to make a difference just because times become tough. Friends, your mind can overcome the mouths of the wicked.

Prepare for Your Opposition's Response

Once the opposition saw that their ridicule did not stop the work, they tried threating them with an attack. On several occasions, the enemies of the reconstruction had received reports that Nehemiah's people were making progress on the wall, but now they received confirmation that the progress was more significant than they had thought. (The gaps were being closed now.) So they conspired together to come to Jerusalem and cause confusion.

This shows us that the enemy will not go down easily. Once you've made your response, you must prepare for them to make their response. Whenever you experience relief from the enemy in one instance, you can't let your guard down because there's another attack in the works.

This is discouraging in itself. The more that you attempt to do what's right, the more the enemy intensifies in their efforts. Nehemiah and his workers applied three simple but effective principles that prepared them for the opposition's response. They prayed together. They positioned themselves so that they could see the oncoming enemies. And they were prepared to fight if necessary. In these three principles, the same truth resonates. Nehemiah did not avoid the attacks but rather adjusted by properly preparing for them. Just as we must prepare to execute our plans, we must also prayerfully prepare for the opposition that may come while we are attempting to execute our plan.

Pronounce Your Need for God's Defense against Your Opposition

Nehemiah instituted an alarm system for those who worked on the wall. Apparently, the workers were scattered all over the wall, and some were so far from one another that they were beyond the reach of the human voice. So when the enemy came near, they merely sounded the trumpet, which signaled all of the people to retreat to the safe spot. Furthermore, this signal just reminded them that they needed God to intervene on their behalf. It did not mean that they were cowards. It just meant that they realized that they needed help from someone that would fight for them. There's nothing wrong with asking someone for help after all.

The citizens of Feldkirch, Austria, didn't know what to do. Napoleon's massive army was preparing to attack. Soldiers had been spotted on the heights above the little town situated on the Austrian border. A council of citizens was hastily summoned to decide whether they should try to defend themselves or surrender. It was Easter Sunday, and the people had gathered in the local church.

The pastor rose and said, "Friends, we have been counting on our own strength, and apparently, that has failed. As this is the day of our Lord's resurrection, let us just ring the bells, have our services as usual, and leave the matter in His hands. We know only our weakness and not the power of God to defend us." The council accepted his plan, and the church bells rang. Hearing the sudden peal, the enemy concluded that the Austrian Army had arrived during the night to defend the town. Before the service ended, the enemy broke camp and left.

That's just the kind of God that we serve. When the enemy is on our trail, God will protect us. Although you may be in the enemy's sights, you're ultimately in God's hands.

CHAPTER
4

How to Defeat Dissension

And there was a great outcry of the people and their wives against their Jewish brethren. For there were those who said, "We, our sons, and our daughters are many; therefore let us get grain, that we may eat and live."

There were also some who said, "We have mortgaged our lands and vineyards and houses, that we might buy grain because of the famine."

There were also those who said, "We have borrowed money for the king's tax on our lands and vineyards.

Yet now our flesh is as the flesh of our brethren, our children as their children; and indeed we are forcing our sons and our daughters to be slaves, and some of our daughters have been brought into slavery. It is not in our power to redeem them, for other men have our lands and vineyards."

And I became very angry when I heard their outcry and these words.

After serious thought, I rebuked the nobles and rulers, and said to them, "Each of you is exacting usury from his brother." So I called a great assembly against them.

And I said to them, "According to our ability we have redeemed our Jewish brethren who were sold to the nations. Now indeed, will you even sell your brethren? Or should they be sold to us?" Then they were silenced and found nothing to say.

Then I said, "What you are doing is not good. Should you not walk in the fear of our God because of the reproach of the nations, our enemies?

I also, with my brethren and my servants, am lending them money and grain. Please, let us stop this usury!

Restore now to them, even this day, their lands, their vineyards, their olive groves, and their houses, also a hundredth of the money and the grain, the new wine and the oil, that you have charged them."

So they said, "We will restore it, and will require nothing from them; we will do as you say." Then I called the priests, and required an oath from them that they would do according to this promise.

Then I shook out the fold of my garment and said, "So may God shake out each man from his house, and from his property, who does not perform this promise. Even thus may he be shaken out and emptied." And all the assembly said, "Amen!" and praised the Lord. Then the people did according to this promise.

Moreover, from the time that I was appointed to be their governor in the land of Judah, from the twentieth year until the thirty-second year of King Artaxerxes, twelve years, neither I nor my brothers ate the governor's provisions.

But the former governors who were before me laid burdens on the people, and took from them bread and wine, besides forty shekels of silver. Yes, even their servants bore rule over the people, but I did not do so, because of the fear of God.

Indeed, I also continued the work on this wall, and we did not buy any land. All my servants were gathered there for the work.

And at my table were one hundred and fifty Jews and rulers, besides those who came to us from the nations around us.

Now that which was prepared daily was one ox and six choice sheep. Also fowl were prepared for me, and once every ten days an abundance of all kinds of wine. Yet in spite of this I did not demand the governor's provisions, because the bondage was heavy on this people.

Remember me, my God, for good, according to all that I have done for this people.

—Nehemiah 5 (NKJV)

Aesop tells a fable of three bulls that fed in a field together. A lion had long watched them in hopes of making them prey but found little chance because they always kept together.

Therefore, he began secretly spreading evil and slanderous reports about each of them against the other until he had stirred up jealousy and distrust among them. Soon, they began to avoid one another, and each took to feeding alone. This gave the lion the opportunity to attack them individually and made easy prey of them all.

Because unresolved dissension and strife existed amongst them, the enemy could come in and both distract and destroy them. That's the result of satanic influence. It takes any opportunity to set up residence in those affected. Often dissension is the result of petty, unresolved tension that has not properly been addressed. And if it's allowed to fester, it has the potential to become toxic.

Dissension affects people from the inside out. Internal frustration develops into an external fight. It begins with a lie here, the slandering of someone's name there, finger pointing here, and blame there. It may begin as something minimal, but eventually, it has the power to turn into something major if it's not resolved.

It's no secret that unity is a powerful staple of the body of Christ, but dissension and disharmony have the power to be doubly damaging. Unity builds, but dissension tears down Unity develops, but dissension destroys. Unity encourages, but dissension discourages.

Teamwork really does make the dream work, but unresolved tension makes for dissension. Whatever you've worked hard to obtain together, dissension can nullify your momentum in one instant. Dissension cannot be ignored. It must be extinguished.

Up to this point, Nehemiah's opposition came from outside of his camp, but now his greatest opposition came from within. All their momentum and hard work was threatened. The closer that they got to the finish line, the wearier they became and the more doubt that they wouldn't be able to finish they felt.

They felt that they had put their lives on hold. Their livelihood had been diminished because they had dedicated so much time to the rebuilding efforts in Jerusalem. Not only were they tired physically and emotionally, but they had basically sacrificed their resources as well. Because of this, they took their minds off the task at hand and started thinking more about their circumstances, and they started blaming one another for their issues.

Now in addition to worrying about the enemy, Nehemiah had to deal with issues from within concerning everyone who had been working toward the common goal. Even though this was devastating for the morale of the group, but he employed the same trust in God that he has used in so many other instances. God would direct him in handling the situation. There was too much at stake for him to allow fighting from within to ruin everything that they had accomplished.

Friends, Satan is too serious of an opponent for us to waste time fighting with one another. Don't give him an opportunity to undo what's already been accomplished. Take note of these three applications.

Consider the Problem

If you factor in the physical and emotional strain of the work, you clearly see the possibility of an inner struggle. They were weary from constantly working, and during the work they were constantly defending themselves against the advances of the enemy. But there was an underlying problem, and the people were not bashful in letting Nehemiah know of their collective and individual issues.

There were three disgruntled groups. First, there were the people who had large families and did not have enough food to eat. The second group had large mortgages to pay and could not buy food. The third group had large taxes to pay and had been forced to mortgage their land. But even worse, they had to sell their children. (This problem was compounded because they had to pay outrageous property taxes to their fellow Jewish brothers who were taking advantage of them.) These were the immediate problems confronting the workers, but the biggest problem the workers faced involved one another.

Poverty and famine were major issues, but the problem didn't escalate until the group started mishandling the money. If you really want to see someone get upset with another individual, make money their primary focus. That's why you must be careful about how you treat others in business affairs. What you do to others could very well come back to you.

But we should focus on something that Nehemiah did here. Before he responded, he first heard them out. He did not interrupt. He merely listened to what they had to say. If he would not have heard them out, he would not have known how to respond. Considering something means that you ponder it in your mind before you react to it. In other words, you must hear and think before you act. Maybe that's why we were blessed with two ears and just one mouth. I truly believe that if we want to effectively resolve conflict, we must listen before we speak. Proverbs 1:5 declares, "A wise man will hear, and will increase learning; and a man of understanding will acquire wise counsel."

But what was Nehemiah's reaction to the problem? It's simple. He was angry, but he was not angry with the people. He was angry about their sins. Deliberate disobedience to the Word of God ought to make us indignant toward sin, but it should not make us indignant toward the sinner. We have a right to be angry about sin, but we should not be angry unto sin.

On many occasions, we are so frustrated by the actions of others in the heat of controversy that we sometimes lose any semblance of patience with individuals. It's so easy to says, "They're never going to grow up. They're not going to change. They're going to continue to do the same things the same way."

That's the easy way out. Although we are to hold individuals accountable, we are to do it with fervent love. First Peter 4:8 (NKJV) records, "And above all things have fervent love for one another, for love will cover a multitude of sins." That word *fervent* is the picture of an athlete stretching out. It is very intense. In this context, it is the picture of people putting for their maximum effort to love their fellow humans. That sounds easy, but here's the catch. If we're going to love like that, it means that our love must go to the extreme, which includes loving those individuals who are not "easy to love." William Barclay says on this topic, "Christian love is not an easy, sentimental reaction. It demands everything a man has of mental and spiritual energy. It means loving even when love isn't reciprocated."

But this is the wonderful thing in the text. Love covers a multitude of sins. Love covers in such a way so that sins aren't swept under the rug, but it covers a variety of sins so that we don't condemn faults but instead forgive those past offenses. Fervent love essentially enables us to avoid condemning others for the very same sins that we've committed and/or are still committing. At the end of the day, we're recipients of the same amazing grace that our generous Savior offers!

Confront the Problem

Before Nehemiah responded to the problem, he spent some time in serious thought, but once he thought about the issue, he publicly rebuked the people. The term *rebuked* was often used by prophets to speak of legal cases brought against guilty people. Sure enough, the people were guilty. They were charging outrageous property taxes, and they were selling their own brethren into slavery. Nehemiah did not hesitate in telling them that what they were doing was not good. They had not only dishonored one another, but they had also dishonored God. Those actions could not go unchallenged.

Don Shula, former coach of the Miami Dolphins, was one day talking to a reporter about a mistake that a player made in practice. He said, "We never allow an error to go unchallenged, because uncorrected errors multiply."

Then the reporter responded, "Isn't there benefit in overlooking one small flaw?"

And Shula responded, "What's a small flaw? I see that all the time with my children. I've allowed a lot of things to slide by because I was too tired or didn't want another confrontation. But you've got to face it someday. You may as well just face them on the spot. If there's something under the surface, you may as well just bring it right out."

In order to be an effective team, we cannot sweep things under the rug. We can't turn a deaf ear to the things we need to address. We can't take a soft stance on hardcore issues. We can't shy away from difficult decisions, and we can't run away from tough choices that affect the well-being of the entire team. We are the standard bearers of society, and if we don't hold one another accountable, then we're not upholding our Christian responsibility. To go a step further, when we don't speak out against wrong, we're allowing someone else to dishonor the God that has been good to us.

Correct the Problem

After reacting and responding to the problem, Nehemiah had to then resolve the problem. He did so by firstly doing what he required of the people. He referred to his own example and others in need by lending them money and grain. He was already doing something about the problem, so he was not asking the people to do something that he was not doing in his own life.

Because he led by example, the others responded accordingly to his exhortation. This is really the heart of the matter. He wanted the people not to just talk about doing better but to take an oath to do better. Nehemiah shook out the folds of his robe to symbolize the fact that God would shake out all of those who had lied to God about doing better for the sake of others and the kingdom.

But there's something to be said about Nehemiah's example. He was proactive in leading the change that he wanted to see. He wanted the people to stop fighting amongst themselves, so he did everything that he could to ensure that things turned for the better.

We can impact the culture of our environment by being the change that we want to see. If you want to experience a more positive culture, you can lead the charge and help infuse positive energy into those around you. Great leaders elevate the thinking and activity of those around them. If you want to see better things, then do better. If you want to experience change, make a change.

CHAPTER
5

Finish What You Start

Now it happened when Sanballat, Tobiah, Geshem the Arab, and the rest of our enemies heard that I had rebuilt the wall, and that there were no breaks left in it (though at that time I had not hung the doors in the gates),

that Sanballat and Geshem sent to me, saying, "Come, let us meet together among the villages in the plain of Ono." But they thought to do me harm.

So I sent messengers to them, saying, "I am doing a great work, so that I cannot come down. Why should the work cease while I leave it and go down to you?"

But they sent me this message four times, and I answered them in the same manner.

Then Sanballat sent his servant to me as before, the fifth time, with an open letter in his hand.

In it was written:

It is reported among the nations, and Geshem says, that you and the Jews plan to rebel; therefore, according to these rumors, you are rebuilding the wall, that you may be their king.

And you have also appointed prophets to proclaim concerning you at Jerusalem, saying, "There is a king in Judah!" Now these matters will be reported to the king. So come, therefore, and let us consult together.

Then I sent to him, saying, "No such things as you say are being done, but you invent them in your own heart."

For they all were trying to make us afraid, saying, "Their hands will be weakened in the work, and it will not be done." Now therefore, O God, strengthen my hands.

Afterward I came to the house of Shemaiah the son of Delaiah, the son of Mehetabel, who was a secret informer; and he said, "Let us meet together in the house of God, within the temple, and let us close the doors of the temple, for they are coming to kill you; indeed, at night they will come to kill you."

And I said, "Should such a man as I flee? And who is there such as I who would go into the temple to save his life? I will not go in!"

Then I perceived that God had not sent him at all, but that he pronounced this prophecy against me because Tobiah and Sanballat had hired him.

For this reason he was hired, that I should be afraid and act that way and sin, so that they might have cause for an evil report, that they might reproach me.

My God, remember Tobiah and Sanballat, according to these their works, and the prophetess Noadiah and the rest of the prophets who would have made me afraid.

So the wall was finished on the twenty-fifth day of Elul, in fifty-two days.

And it happened, when all our enemies heard of it, and all the nations around us saw these things, that they were very disheartened in their own eyes; for they perceived that this work was done by our God.

Also in those days the nobles of Judah sent many letters to Tobiah, and the letters of Tobiah came to them.

For many in Judah were pledged to him, because he was the son-in-law of Shechaniah the son of Arah, and his son Jehohanan had married the daughter of Meshullam the son of Berechiah.

Also they reported his good deeds before me, and reported my words to him. Tobiah sent letters to frighten me.

—Nehemiah 6 (NKJV)

J. Stowell talks about how the Greeks had a very unique race in their Olympic games. The winner was not the runner who finished first, but rather it was the runner who finished with the torch still lit in his hand. Everyone involved wanted to run all the way with the flame still burning on their torch. It wasn't so important how they started the race but rather how they finished.

And in our day and age, we often see people *never* finish what they start. We see college students who complete one or two years of college coursework, spend thousands of dollars on tuition, but never complete their degrees. We witness individuals begin jobs, receive adequately training, but never complete the first year of employment. At the beginning of each year, we make all types of resolutions and goals with good intentions but often never finish these.

We often have the zeal to start, but for whatever reason—maybe because of difficulties or adversities along the way—we don't have the endurance to finish. Many individuals don't quit as soon as they begin, but instead they quit with success in view. In other words, people do not quit at the starting line but right before they get to the finish line.

This world is full of great starters but lacks many great finishers. What this world and what the kingdom needs is more individuals who do not become discouraged and disheartened by the obstacles they face, people who don't succumb to the wicked ploys of the enemy before they realize success. We need those who will stay the course until they achieve their assigned tasks.

Nehemiah and his team of workers were on the brink of completing the rebuilding project in Jerusalem, and now he only had to open the gates. But when Tobiah, Sanballat, and Geshem heard that the seemingly impossible work was almost complete—all except for hanging a few doors on the gates—they became quite angry and sought to stop the work and kill Nehemiah by luring him to the village Ono.

But Nehemiah let them know that he could not and would not meet them because he was diligent in finishing his mission. This was not some ordinary work that he was adamant about completing. This was a God-commissioned work that he would finish at any cost.

And I believe that same type of zeal is warranted even for us in modern days. God is calling for those who are committed to carry out any task for His cause, no matter what the obstacles may be. If you have the faith to finish one of God's goal, He will help you complete it, no matter what opposition or obstacles are. If He's given you the command to start, He'll give you the courage to finish.

Determination

The mere fact that Nehemiah had nearly finished his task of rebuilding the walls in a short period of fifty-two days—despite so much adversity, disappointment, and so many obstacles—never wavering from his true purpose, shows that he was a determined man.

To add to his difficulties, he was faced with a personal attack on his work and his life by three men who sought to end everything he had devoted himself to. (After all he had been through, he only had one small but important part of the project remaining to complete.) The fact that Nehemiah did not cower at the first glimpse of difficulty and dismay, whether it was a result of circumstances or evil forces, is a testament of his great determination.

Nehemiah would not let anything or anyone stop him from doing what he had set out to do. He had made it this far, and there would be no stopping him from completing the work. Determined people keep pressing on, no matter what the obstacles or the opposition may suggest.

We must adopt that same spirit of determination. In this life and in the work of the kingdom, we will be confronted with all types of adversity and obstacles, but we must stay the course and face our difficulties head-on. That's what determination really is—being strong in character and disciplined enough to hang tough in the face of insurmountable odds. In order for us to see a great work through to completion, we need determination because it stirs our hope and keeps us positive throughout the duration of our work.

The days ahead will be filled with many trials and treacherous circumstances, both inside and outside of these four walls, and at times it will seem easier to quit, but we cannot allow the disappointments on the outside to ruin the determination that we possess on the inside.

In order for us to soar to higher heights and grander ventures, we need more individuals who are not afraid to pursue excellence in the face of the opposition, people who are not afraid to stay in the race when it is easier to just throw in the towel and wave the white flag of surrender, people who will not back down when others say that they can't win, people who will not buckle under pressure, people who will not cave in when the challenges of life and ministry become great. In short, we need more determined people. God will make the difference!

Distraction-Free Demeanor

When Nehemiah's people were about to complete the work, these three men sent messengers that told him that they wanted to meet him in Ono. They had already tried to halt the rebuilding project several times before, but this time they took their attacks to another level. They literally wanted to lure him away from Jerusalem and kill him.

By removing him from the scene or at least destroying his credibility with the Jews, they thought could either cease the work or eliminate Nehemiah (if not both). If they could only draw him away from Jerusalem, then he could not oversee the work. Plus they wanted to kill him away from his home. They had sent the invitation four different times, but each time Nehemiah gave the same refusal. He was too focused on the work at hand to become distracted by those who wanted to hinder his progress.

Then Nehemiah's opposition tried one more time to stop the work. Sanballat sent his servant to Nehemiah with an unsealed letter that reported an alleged rumor that Nehemiah was trying to set himself as the next king of the Jews, which would have made him a direct threat to King Artexerxes, the man who had made the rebuilding project a reality. (He wanted people who read the unsealed letter to spread the news and implicate Nehemiah.)

Nehemiah boldly denied the accusations and told his fellow workers that the letter was designed to frighten them with the king's wrath and to encourage them to quit and leave the rest of the work undone. Those guys just wouldn't stop.

We must ready ourselves for all types of distractions. Satan is always going to do whatever he has to do to destroy the followers of God and oppose anything or anyone associated with God. Even if we aren't distracted, we cannot let down our guards. If he cannot get us one way, he will try using anything or anyone to get us another way. We cannot be numb and unconscious to the tactics of Satan because he never slacks off at his job. He is literally waiting to devour whomever he can.

During my undergraduate degree at Austin College, I was on the football team. At the beginning of each week, we received a scouting report, and we were also required to watch a certain amount of game film on our upcoming opponent. This report was useful because it listed all of the tendancies of our opponents in every possible situation, so when we watched the film, we could adequately prepare for whatever the opponent threw at us. There were even times when the scout team threw trick plays into the game plan, but because we were adequately prepared, the opponent didn't overwhelm us with their strategies. It is imperative that we raise our level of awareness about Satan and his tactics.

We should not only be aware of the tactics of the enemy, but we should resist him by developing a distraction-free demeanor that declares, "I don't have time to come down to where you are because I am doing great work for God and I have no time for distractions or distracting people." Simply put, we can only develop a distraction-free demeanor when we don't tolerate foolishness. Just as the wall was used as a means of restriction and protection, we should set up walls in our lives that will restrict distractions.

One cannot be elevated while still weighed down by hindrances. If we want to be better than we were in the past, we cannot allow the same distractions that hindered us then to distract us now. Frankly, we must develop a demeanor that literally blocks our distractions.

That is the context of this particular narrative, but, metaphorically, for so many of us, there's also a threat for us to "come down" from the wall of integrity and consult with immorality. Sin constantly nips at us on all fronts. There's always a distraction that looks to bring us down and compromise our morals. Tempation is always present, feeding into those sinful distractions.

For the believer, temptation is a mighty foe. Though trials are used to develop spiritual maturity, temptation comes to obstruct spiritual maturity. F. P. Wood so eloquently said, "Temptation in itself is not sin; rather it is the call to battle against sin. The point is that we are in a war, a continual war against our soul, and it is not simply a momentary skirmish. Our flesh, the evil world system, and the evil one are resolutely determined to take us down!" Temptation is a battle that we must fight, but it's a war that we cannot afford to lose.

Divine Assistance

Nehemiah's enemies were desperate. None of their ploys had worked. All throughout the rebuilding effort, while the enemy attempted to distract, discourage, and destroy, the workers kept on working. But Nehemiah understood that he and his workers could complete the work *and* handle their enemies without the assistance of someone greater than their enemies.

So he did what he knew was best in a time of crisis. He prayed and asked that God would strengthen his and his workers' hands so that they could finally complete their task. This confidence in God's strength held Nehemiah and his team together from start to finish. They continually trusted God for strength in times of weakness. What an awesome principle! There is nothing wrong with depending on the Lord. When we cry out to Him to strengthen our hands, He will do so.

Make no mistake about it. The divine assistance from our heavenly Father gives us the extra assistance that we need to complete *any* task and cross the finish line.

In the 1992 Olympics in Barcelona, the four-hundred-meter favorite, Derek Redmond, was approaching the homestretch and literally tore both of his hamstrings. He lay there in a pool of his own misery, disappointed and defeated, as all of the other participants finished the race before him. Determined to finish the race, he attempted to finish the race under his own power, but he was physically unable to do so.

In the crowd you could hear a huge commotion. An elderly man pushed through security so that he could walk on the track where

Redmond was lying. This elderly man turned out to be Redmond's father, and he volunteered to help Redmond cross the finish line. In one of the most heartfelt scenes in Olympic history, a father helped his son finish the race that he had started. Friends, you have a heavenly Father that will help you overcome all obstacles and finish that which you have started. With God's help, you can begin again and also finish.

Horatio Palmer so eloquently put the following words to music:

> Yield not to temptation, for yielding is sin.
> Each vict'ry will help you some other to win.
> Fight manfully onward, dark passions subdue.
> Look ever to Jesus. He'll carry you through.
>
> Ask the Savior to help you,
> Comfort, strengthen, and keep you.
> He is willing to aid you.
> He will carry you through.
>
> Shun evil companions, bad language disdain,
> God's name hold in rev'rence, nor take it in vain.
> Be thoughtful and earnest, kindhearted and true.
> Look ever to Jesus. He'll carry you through.
>
> To him that o'ercometh, God giveth a crown.
> Through faith we will conquer, though often cast down.
> He who is our Savior, our strength will renew.
> Look ever to Jesus. He'll carry you through.

Printed in the United States
By Bookmasters